GOLF

Don Wells

WEIGL PUBLISHERS INC.

Published by Weigl Publishers Inc.

350 5th Avenue, Suite 3304, PMB 6G

New York, NY USA 10118-0069

www.weigl.com

Copyright 2006 Weigl Publishers Inc.

Library of Congress Cataloging-in-Publication Data

Wells, Don.

  For the love of golf / by Don Wells.

     p. cm. -- (For the love of sports)

  Includes index.

  ISBN 1-59036-296-9 (hard cover : alk. paper) -- ISBN 1-59036-300-0 (soft cover : alk. paper)

  1. Golf--Juvenile literature. I. Title. II. Series.

  GV968.W45 2006

  796.352--dc22

                              2004029147

Printed in the United States of America

1 2 3 4 5 6 7 8 9 09 08 07 06 05

Project Coordinator

Tina Schwartzenberger

Substantive Editor

Frances Purslow

Copy Editor

Heather C. Hudak

Design

Warren Clark

Layout

Kathryn Livingstone

Photo Researcher

Kim Winiski

Contents

All About Golf

Golf is a game played on a large, outdoor field called a course. A course can have nine or eighteen holes. Players use a club to hit a small ball into each hole. The goal of the game is to use as few strokes, or hits, as possible to sink the ball into the hole. Players finish the game when they have sunk the ball into all the holes on the course.

The game of golf began in the Scottish Kingdom of Fife in the 1300s or 1400s. Players hit a pebble around a grassy course that had sand **dunes**, rabbit holes, and animal trails. The Gentlemen Golfers of Leith was the first **golf club**. It formed in 1744 for a golf **competition**. First prize was a silver golf club.

The Royal Burgess Golfing Society of Edinburgh in Scotland played golf on Bruntsfield Links, in the shadow of Edinburgh Castle.

More than 26 million Americans play golf at least once each year.

St. Andrews golf club in Scotland is considered the birthplace of modern golf. The club created rules and **promoted** golf as a proper sport. Golf was first played at St. Andrews in 1552. The St. Andrews Society of Golfers formed in 1754. This golf club held a tournament each year. The first women's golf club formed at St. Andrews in 1895.

In the early 1800s, people made golf clubs by hand. They were too costly for most people to buy. Soon, factories began making golf equipment. Factories could make the equipment quickly. It was less costly to buy. More people began playing golf. Golf is now played in almost every country in the world.

St. Andrews in Scotland was the first 18-hole golf course.

CHECK IT OUT

Learn about golf's beginnings at

www.learnaboutgolf.com/ educational/history.html

Getting Ready to Play

Golfers need special equipment to play the game. They wear different types of clothing while playing golf. Most players wear casual shirts and pants that allow them to move freely when swinging the golf club.

Players wear loose, comfortable pants and shirts with collars.

Some players wear shoes with spikes. Spikes stop players from slipping when they swing the club.

A player needs golf clubs and a golf ball to play the game. There are three types of clubs. They are woods, irons, and putters. Woods are the longest clubs. They have a large head and are used to hit the ball hundreds of yards down the course. There are many different irons. Irons with a low number, such as a three iron, are used to hit the ball long distances. High number irons, such as the 9 iron, are used to hit the ball short distances. Players use these irons when the ball is near the **green**. Players use putters on the green to hit the ball a short distance into the hole.

The first golf balls were made of wood. In the 1600s, players began using feather balls. They were popular. Today, golfers can choose from two types of golf balls. One type is made of a solid **core**. The core is wound with rubber and covered with balata. Balata is a soft material. Players can make the balata golf ball spin on the green and move to the left or right. The other type of golf ball has a solid core covered by surlyn. Surlyn is a strong material that does not nick or cut. Many players do not use surlyn-covered balls because they are more difficult to make spin or move to the left or right.

Players wear sunscreen for protection from the Sun. Some players also wear hats.

The golf bag is used to carry equipment, such as golf clubs and golf balls.

Golfers use scorecards to keep track of the number of times they hit the ball.

The Golf Course

Golf courses are divided into sections called holes. Most 18-hole courses are about 6,500 to 7,000 yards (5,900 to 6,400 meters) long. Each hole has a starting point known as a **tee**. The golfer hits the ball off the tee, toward the hole. The hole is marked by a flag. It shows players where to aim the ball. A metal or plastic cup is inside the hole. The distance between the tee and the hole is between 100 and 600 yards (90 and 550 m).

When players hit the ball off the tee, they aim for an area of short grass called the fairway. On either side of the fairway is an area with long grass, bushes, or trees called the rough. It is difficult to hit the ball long distances in the rough.

There are more than 16,000 golf courses in the United States.

Golf courses also have hazards. Ditches and bunkers are hazards. Hazards are sand traps, or low areas filled with sand. Water hazards are streams, creeks, ponds, and lakes.

An area of very short grass around the cup is called the putting green. It is easier for a player to roll the ball into the cup on this short grass.

Golfers began using reusable tees around 1900. Before tees were available, golfers created temporary tees using piles of sand.

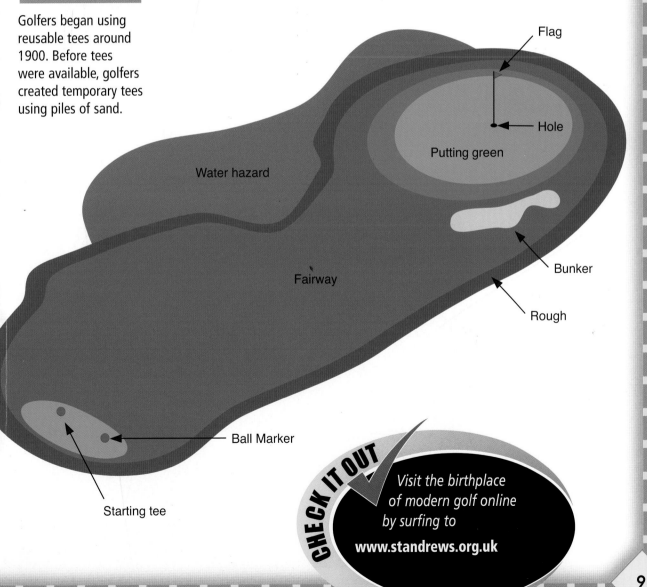

Flag

Hole

Putting green

Water hazard

Bunker

Fairway

Rough

Ball Marker

Starting tee

CHECK IT OUT

Visit the birthplace of modern golf online by surfing to

www.standrews.org.uk

Game Basics

Most golf rules are the same for men and women. During a round, or game, of golf, a player is allowed to carry up to 14 different clubs.

Two to four people usually play a round of golf. Play begins at each hole with a player hitting, or driving, the ball onto the fairway. Players walk or ride in a golf cart to the place where the ball lands.

Players must hit the ball from wherever it lands. This is called the lie of the ball. Players may need to hit the ball many times before it reaches the hole. A golfer's score is the total number of strokes used to move the ball from the tee to the cup.

Some people use golf carts to travel between the holes. They can also store their clubs in the cart while playing the game.

Golfers cannot move the ball before they hit it. Sometimes reaching the ball is difficult.

Each golf course has a par. Par is the average number of strokes used to complete a hole. Par depends on the distance between the tee and the cup. The pars for each hole add up to par for the entire course. Par for most 18-hole golf courses is between 70 and 72. Professional golfers score in the 60s and low 70s. The winner of a golf game is the person who used the lowest number of strokes to complete the game.

Some **amateur** golfers can drive the ball more than 200 yards (183 m) from the tee onto the fairway. They can reach the green using fewer than three strokes. This is because the farther they drive the ball, the closer it lands to the hole. Professional golfers can drive the ball much further than amateurs can.

A driving range is an area where golfers can practice hitting balls and try to perfect their swings.

Large scoreboards called leader boards track the top players at major competitions.

LEADERS

PRIOR	HOLE	1	2	3	4	5	6	7	8	9	10	11	12	13	14	15	16	17	18
	PAR	4	5	4	3	4	3	4	5	4	4	4	3	5	4	5	3	4	4
0	RILEY	1	1	1	0	0	0	0	0	0	0	0	0	0	0	1	1	1	2
0	CEJKA	0	1	2	2	2	2	1	1	1	1	2	1	1	1	2	2	2	2
0	HOWELL III	0	0	0	0	1	1	1	1	1	1	1	1	0	0	1	1	1	1
0	LANGER	1	1	0	0	1	0	0	0	0	0	0	0	1	1	1	2	1	1
0	PRICE N.	0	1	1	0	0	0	1	1	1	1	1	1	1	1	1	2	0	0
0	ROSE	1	2	2	2	2	2	2	2	3	3	2	2	3	3	3	3	4	5
0	ELS	0	1	1	1	1	1	1	2	2	2	3	2	2	2	3	3	2	2
0	DiMARCO	0	0	0	0	0	2	2	2	2	2	2	2	2	2	3	3	3	3
0	CLARKE	1	1	1	1	1	1	1	1	1	1	0	0	1	1	2	2	1	2
0	HAAS J.	1	2	2	2	1	1	2	2	2	2	2	3	3	3	3	3	3	3

THRU 16

WOODS	3
WITTENBERG	4
BJORN	7

Golf Shots

Golfers use special words to describe their scores. Completing a hole using one stroke less than par is called a birdie. Completing a hole using two strokes less than par is called an eagle. A bogey is a score of one more stroke than par. Hitting the ball into the cup with one stroke is called a hole in one. A hole in one is rare.

There are three types of shots used to play each hole. The first shot is called the drive. This is a long shot from the tee. The second shot is called the approach shot. This shot is used to hit the ball onto the green. The third type of shot is the putt. A golfer putts the ball a short distance into the cup to complete the hole.

An approach shot is usually much shorter in distance than a drive.

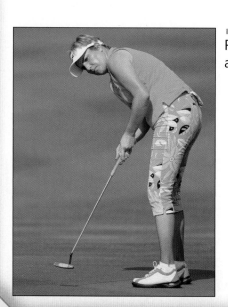

Putting requires a large amount of concentration.

Many players use the driver to hit the ball as hard as possible. They believe this will make the ball travel farther. This is not true. To travel far, they must hit the ball using proper **techniques**.

Not all greens are flat. The ball travels at various speeds on different greens. A good putter watches how the dips and slopes on a green affect how the ball travels. The putter can change the technique they use when hitting the ball on the green.

Many golfers spend a great deal of time lining up a putt.

Golfers must learn when to use a wood (top), iron (middle), and putter (bottom).

CHECK IT OUT

Get some pointers from professional golfers by visiting

www.pgaprofessional. com/golf_tips.html

Golf Etiquette

Golfers must be polite and **courteous** when they play golf. Golf **etiquette** ensures that all players enjoy their round of golf. Here are some rules of golf etiquette.

Golf requires concentration. Players should not talk or move around when another player is making a shot.

A player who putts or **chips** the ball near the hole can take his or her next turn immediately. If the golfer waits for his or her next turn, he or she must pick up the ball and mark its position with a coin or **ball-marker**. A ball left near the cup can **distract** other players when they are putting.

Golfers waiting to take their turn should stand quietly behind and off to the side of the person taking a shot.

Players should not walk through bunkers. Footprints can affect how the ball bounces in the bunker. Players must always rake away their footprints and ball marks as they leave a bunker.

Players should never stand on the lip of the cup to retrieve their ball. This causes the lip to collapse, or fall in, and can affect other players' putts.

Slower golfers should allow faster golfers to "play through" or take their turns ahead of their group. Players in groups of two or more can begin play on a hole before a golfer playing alone. On par 4 and 5 holes, players should tee off after each player in the group ahead has taken at least two shots. On par 3 holes, players must wait until the group ahead has moved off the green before teeing off.

Coins or ball-markers mark the ball's position near the hole.

CHECK IT OUT

To learn more basic golf etiquette, surf to

http://partners.golf serv.com/apps/tools/ etiquette.asp

15

Where the Action Is

The Royal and Ancient Golf Club of St. Andrews and the United States Golf Association (USGA) **govern** golf. Male professional golfers belong to the Professional Golfers' Association of America (PGA). Female professional golfers belong to the Ladies Professional Golf Association (LPGA). Most professional golfers work as instructors at clubs or **resorts**. The PGA Tour hosts professional men's tournaments. The LPGA hosts professional women's tournaments.

There are thousands of golf tournaments each year. The most important professional men's tournaments are the Masters, the U.S. Open, the British Open, and the PGA Championship. These four tournaments are known as the grand slam of golf. The most important amateur tournaments for men are the U.S. Amateur and the British Amateur. Both amateur and professional golfers can play in the U.S. Open and the British Open.

The team that wins the World Amateur Team Championship receives the Eisenhower Trophy.

The four most important professional women's tournaments are the LPGA Championship, the U.S. Women's Open, the Women's British Open, and the Nabisco Championship. These tournaments are the women's grand slam of golf. The most important amateur tournaments for women are the U.S. Women's Amateur and the British Women's Amateur championships.

Male and female professional golfers look forward to the PGA and LPGA Championships. Each year, the PGA Championship is held at a different American golf course. The LPGA tournament stays at the same course for several years before changing location. Only professional golfers may play in the PGA and LPGA Championships. The PGA was created in 1916 and held its first championship in 1955. The first LPGA Championship was also in 1955.

Every 2 years, male amateur golfers from the United States play against golfers from England, Ireland, Scotland, and Wales for the Walker Cup.

The Curtis Cup Match is a women's tournament between the United States and Great Britain.

Golf Superstars

Many people enjoy watching golf. Golf stars are always breaking records and amazing fans.

JACK NICKLAUS

BIRTH DATE:
January 21, 1940
HOMETOWN:
Columbus, Ohio

Career Facts:

- Nicklaus has won 70 PGA events in the United States.
- Nicklaus has won 20 major tournaments.
- Nicklaus has won two U.S. Amateur championships, six Masters championships, four U.S. Open championships, five U.S. PGA Championships, and three British Open championships.
- Nicklaus has represented the United States in six Ryder Cup tournaments. This tournament is held every two years for professional men's golf teams in the United States and Europe.
- Nicklaus is known as "the Golden Bear."
- Nicklaus has designed golf courses, including Castle Pines Golf Club in Castle Rock, Colorado.

ELDRICK (TIGER) WOODS

BIRTH DATE:
December 30, 1975
HOMETOWN:
Cypress, California

Career Facts:

- Woods has won 53 tournaments around the world and earned almost $50 million.
- Woods has won eight major championships. He has won three Masters championships, two U.S. Open championships, two U.S. PGA Championships, and one British Open championship.
- Woods holds the record for lowest score in the Masters, U.S. Open, and British Open.
- Woods shares the record for the lowest score at the U.S. Open. Woods scored 272 in 2000. Woods's idol, Jack Nicklaus, first scored 272 in 1980. Lee Janzen matched the score in 1993.
- Woods has been PGA Player of the Year six times—1997, 1999, 2000, 2001, 2002, and 2003.
- Woods was ranked number one golfer in the world for a record 264 weeks.

BOBBY JONES

BIRTH DATE:
March 17, 1902
HOMETOWN:
Atlanta, Georgia

Career Facts:

- Jones is widely considered to be the greatest amateur golfer of modern times.

- Jones is the only player to win four major championships in the same year. In 1930, he won the British Amateur, the British Open, the U.S. Amateur, and the U.S. Open.

- Jones won one British Amateur championship, three British Open championships, five U.S. Amateur championships, and four U.S. Open championships.

- Jones played on the 1922, 1924, 1926, 1928, and 1930 U.S. Walker Cup teams. He won nine of ten matches.

- Jones helped to design the golf course for the Masters championship. This annual event was first held in 1934, at the Augusta National Golf Club in Georgia.

PATTY BERG

BIRTH DATE:
February 13, 1918
HOMETOWN:
Minneapolis, Minnesota

Career Facts:

- Berg was the Associated Press Female Athlete of the Year in 1938, 1943, and 1955.

- Berg turned professional in 1940.

- Berg helped found the Ladies Professional Golf Association. In 1949, she became its first president. Her term lasted until 1952.

- Berg won the first U.S. Women's Open championship in 1946.

- Berg won 57 professional tournaments, including 15 major championships, during her career.

- Berg is a member of the LPGA Hall of Fame, International Women's Sports Hall of Fame, PGA Hall of Fame, University of Minnesota Hall of Fame, American, Minnesota, and Florida Sports Halls of Fame. She is one of only two women in the PGA Golf Hall of Fame.

CHECK IT OUT

Find out more about members of the World Golf Hall of Fame at www.wgv.com/hof/members.html

Health and Fitness

Golf does not look like it takes a great deal of energy to play. Still, players twist, stretch, and bend many times during a round of golf. To get the most out of golf, players must eat a healthy diet.

Fruits and vegetables provide many of the vitamins needed to remain healthy. Breads, pasta, and rice are sources of food energy. Meats have protein for building muscles. Dairy products have calcium, which keeps bones strong. Eating foods from all the food groups every day will keep a golfer's body healthy and in good shape.

Drinking plenty of water before, during, and after playing golf is important. Water keeps golfer's bodies cool.

Most Americans should eat seven servings of fruits and vegetables every day.

Golfers need to drink plenty of water to replace what their bodies lose through sweat.

CHECK IT OUT

Learn more about eating well by visiting **www.usda.gov/cnpp**

S trong, **flexible** muscles are important for playing golf. Training the right muscles a few times every week makes playing golf more fun and prevents injuries. Stretching keeps muscles flexible. It is best to stretch during and after a **warm up**.

Golfers need strong back muscles. A simple weight-training program strengthens back muscles. Many players feel strong back muscles help them hit the ball longer distances. Strong back muscles also help players avoid back injuries.

Golfers twist many times during a golf game. Stretching prevents injuries.

Some golfers stretch during games to keep their muscles flexible.

21

Golf Brain Teasers

Test your knowledge of this sport by trying to answer these golf brain teasers!

Q Where is the birthplace of modern golf?

A St. Andrews, Scotland, is considered the birthplace of modern golf.

Q What does a player need to play golf?

A A player needs a set of golf clubs and a golf ball to play a round of golf.

Q What type of course was used when golf was first played?

A Players hit a pebble around a grassy course that had sand dunes, rabbit holes, and animal trails.

Q What is the starting point of a hole called?

A The starting point of a golf hole is called the tee.

Q Where does a golfer use a putter?

A Golfers use a putter on the green.

Q What are the most important tournaments in professional men's golf?

A The Masters, the U.S. Open, the British Open, and the PGA Championship are the most important tournaments.

Glossary

amateur: a person who is not paid to play a game and who may not have much experience

ball-marker: a small plastic disk

chips: shots that raise the ball, and are played around the green

competition: a contest or game

core: the center

courteous: polite

distract: to draw a person's attention away from what they are doing

dunes: a mound or ridge of sand

etiquette: rules of correct behavior

flexible: able to bend

golf club: a group of people who play golf on the same course; also, the stick used to hit a golf ball

govern: to rule

green: the area of very short grass around the cup

promoted: encouraged the growth and development or popularity

resorts: places people go for fun or relaxation

techniques: practical ways to perform a particular task or art

tee: a peg placed in the ground to hold a golf ball

warm up: gentle exercise to get a person's body ready for stretching and game play

Index